CATS GETTING STUCK!

Get meowta here!

EBURY
PRESS

5 7 9 10 8 6

Ebury Press, an imprint of Ebury Publishing
20 Vauxhall Bridge Road
London SW1V 2SA

Ebury Press is part of the Penguin Random House group of companies
whose addresses can be found at global.penguinrandomhouse.com

Copyright © Ebury Press 2017
Photo research and captions by Mathew Growcoot

First published by Ebury Press in 2017

www.penguin.co.uk

A CIP catalogue record for this book is available from the British Library

ISBN 9781785036309

Printed and bound in Italy by Printer Trento S.r.l.

Feeling a bit cagey about this!

I need to think outside the box!

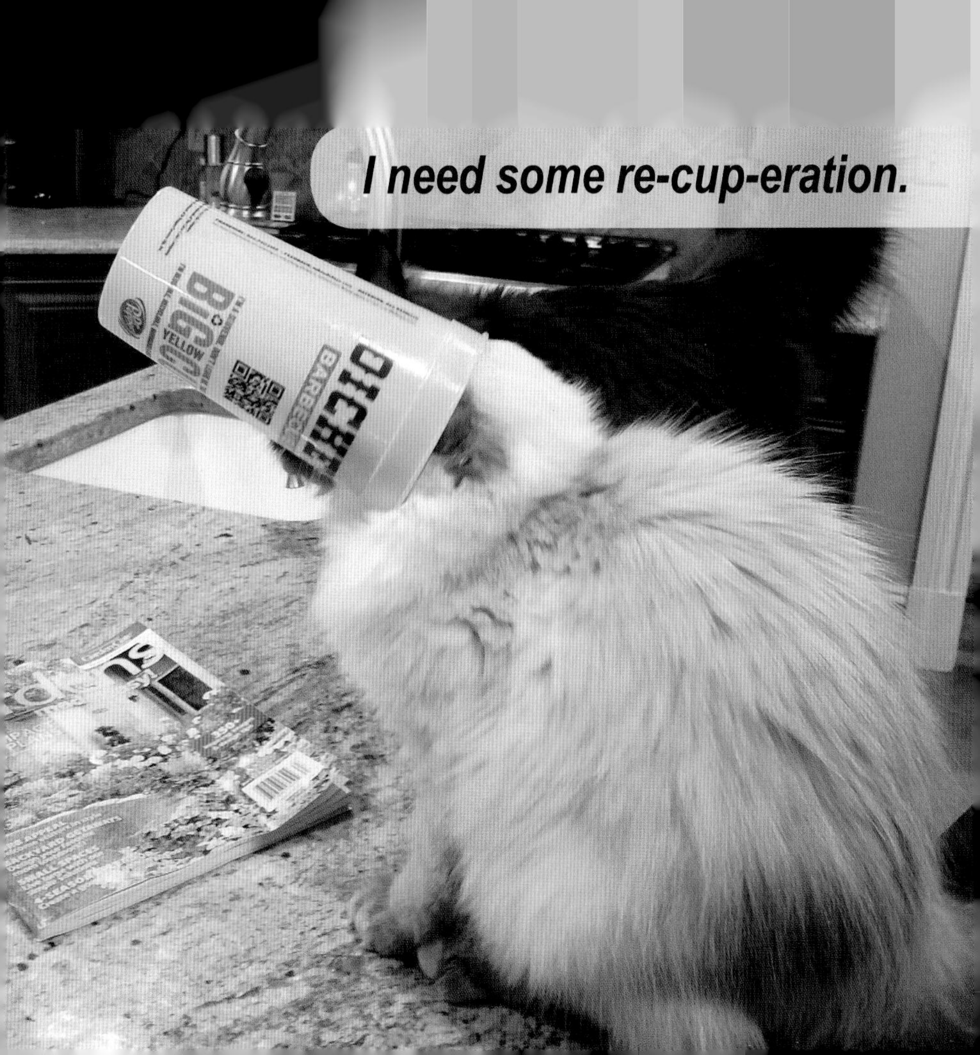
I need some re-cup-eration.

This could be cat-astrophic!

Cat's not the way to do it!

Introducing: a diapurr!

Come on baby, let's go for a spin.

I'm just gonna hole up here.

Wood you believe it?!

I may have miss-cat-ulated the situation.

Hiss-washer.

Cat you help me out?

Any-fin is possible.

What a great car-pet!

Will somebody call the purrlice?

How dairy drink my milk!

I'll get you e-vent-ually...

It's looking rather purr-carious.

Kitten Impossible.

One must question this cat's frame of mind.

I've been cornered.

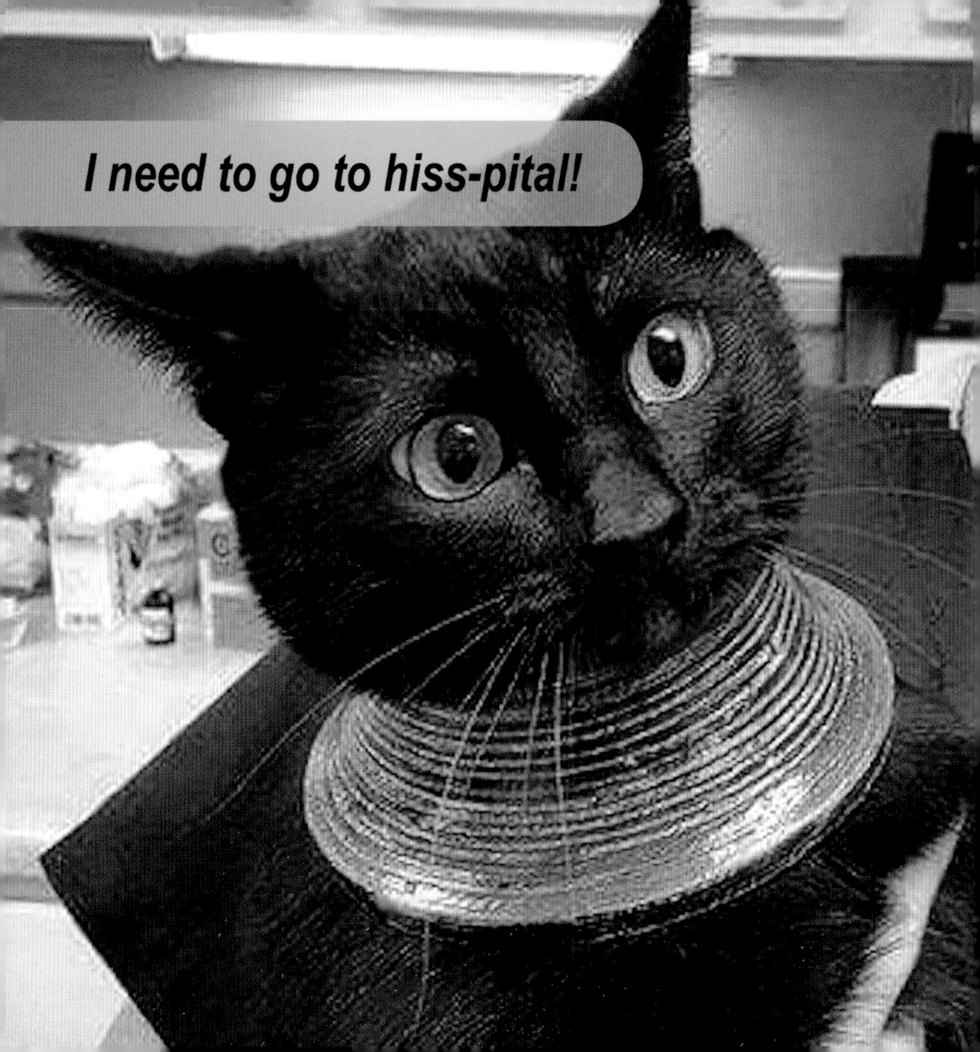
I need to go to hiss-pital!

I can't handle this...

It's all getting a bit hairy.

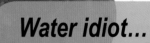

PASSPORT APP. +
DRIVING LICENCE

I'll be filing a claim because of this.

Hello Kitty!

Get meowta here!

This is paw-ful!

Feeling flush!

Is that you, Santa Claws?

I'm knit getting out of this one!

I've been bowl-ed over!

I need a get-out claws.

Feeling a bit cat-hletic.

Do you find this ameowsing?

This is a deli-cat situation.

I've bagged a winner!

Causing of-fence.

I might need a purramedic.

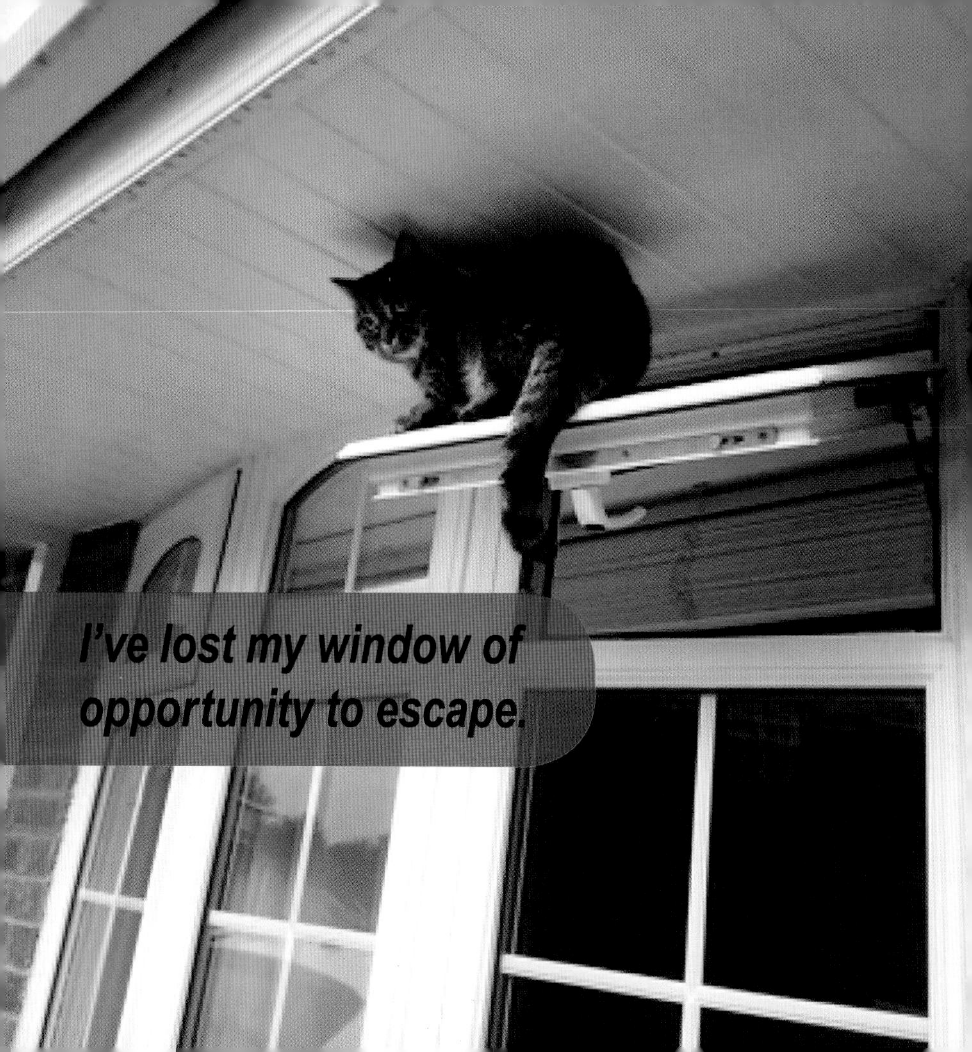
I've lost my window of opportunity to escape.

Let the cat out of the bag.

Sofa so good!

No cat is an island... except this one.

Diamonds are a cat's best friend.

A little help, purrlease!

Totally floored.

Get me out right meow!

Pearl

Let's make sweet meowsic.

Reference
Head by REMO

I've been a bag kitty.

Sometimes it's good to paws for thought.

Can't see the puss for the trees.

Life's a balancing act...

Feline a bit stupid here...

It's curtains for me!

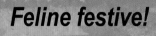
Feline festive!

This is a little jarring to my nerves.

Barking up the wrong tree.

What a pane!

Meow do I look?

This is snow joke!

Living life on the ledge!

This is meshing me up.

Cats on a hot tin roof.

This is furry embarrassing...

Feline stumped!

Let's get down to the knitty gritty.

Santa Claws is coming to town!

Just one step at a time...

Trying out the fur-sbury flop.

Human, I request your assistance.

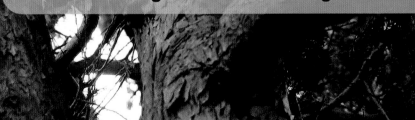

I'm branching off to something new.

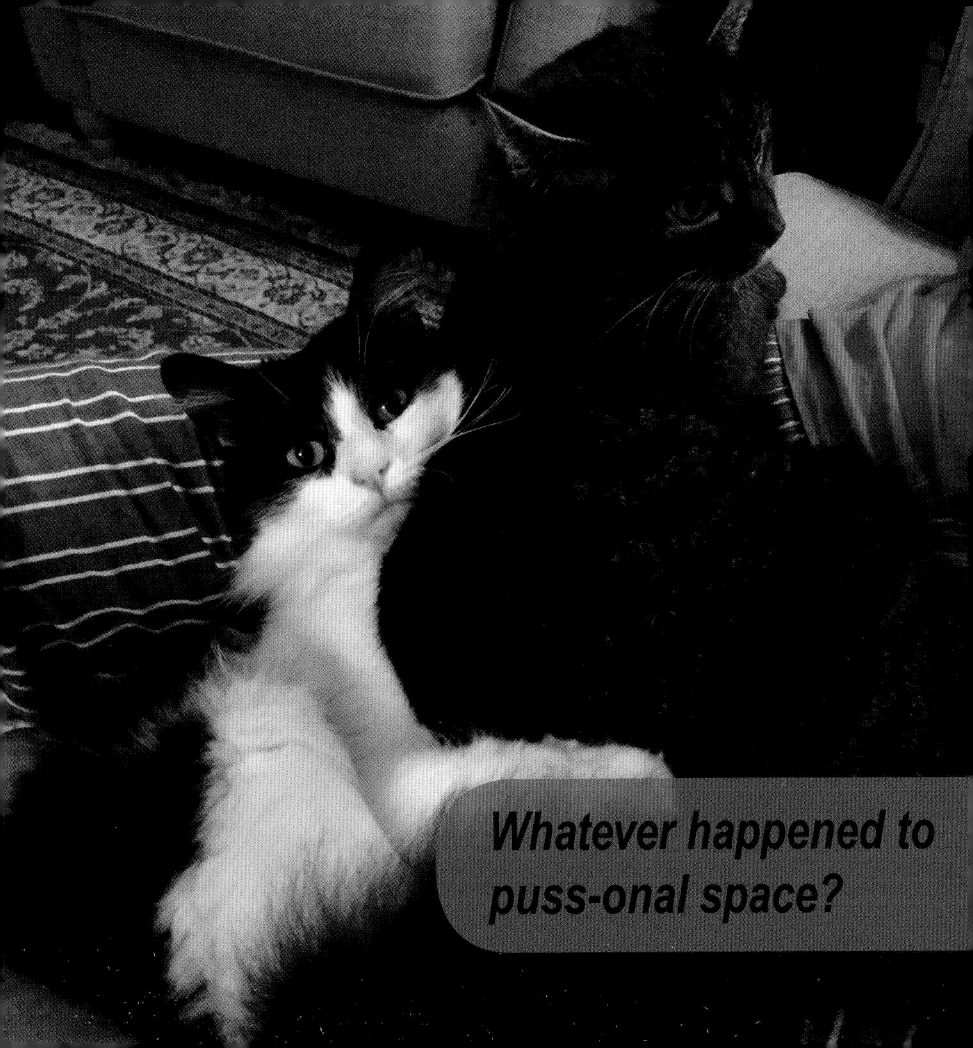
Whatever happened to puss-onal space?

Leaf me alone, I know what I'm doing.

One clever kit-tin.

A tree-mendously stupid idea.

Paws for reflection.

This cat is known for being spiky...

Cat got your tongue?

Unhook me right meow!

A cautionary tail.

Sliding Paws.

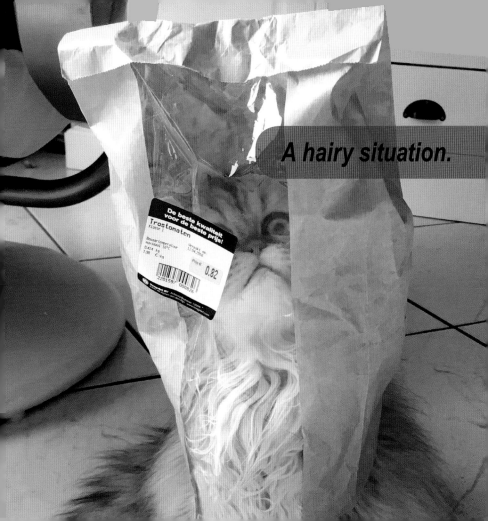

A hairy situation.

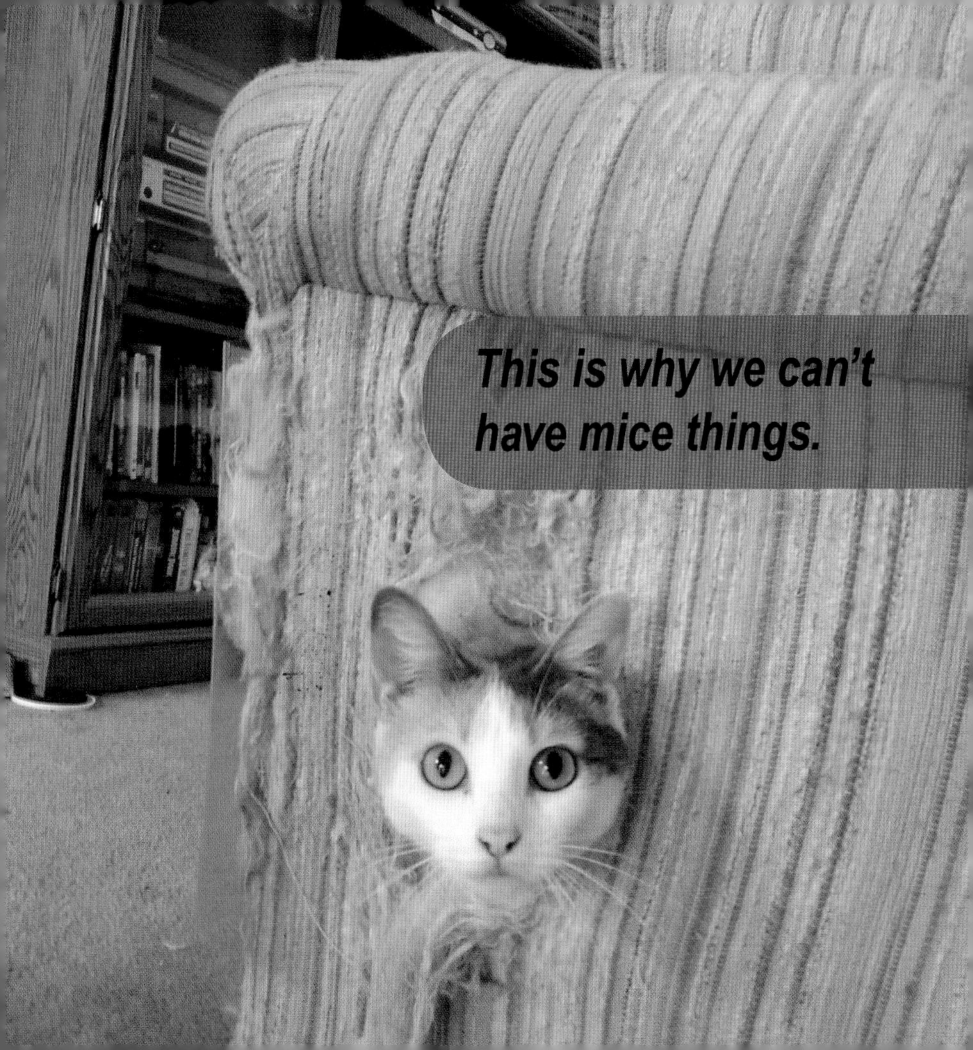
This is why we can't
have mice things.

Aisle be watching you...

This cat needs to stop fan-nying around.

Clothes don't maketh the cat.

Are you furr-real?

Merry Hiss-mas!

I've bin a bad kitty...

Creature discomforts.

This was a bird-brained idea.

Today I will be stuck to the sofa.

Feline the squeeze…

Cat makes a splash!

A truly domestic cat.

I want to bring the curtain down on this situation.

I think I better leave right meow.

I think someone had planted a trap.

Make mine a cream liqueur.

Meowy Christmas!

Feline boxed-in.

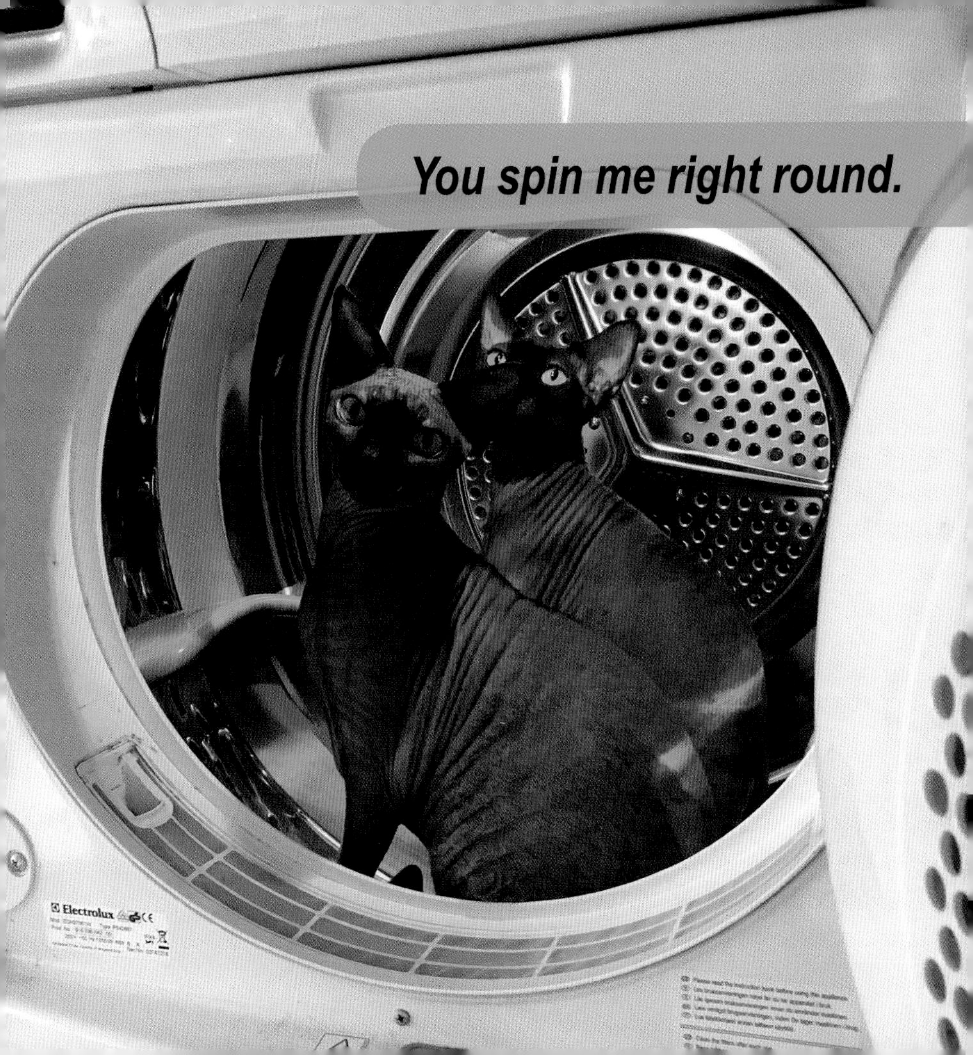
You spin me right round.
Electrolux

This is taking the puss.

Pets beginning to look a lot like Christmas!

I have an excellent shelf-life.

I jumped in, feet last.

Photo credits